THE *soul* AFLAME

THE *soul* AFLAME
a modern book of hours

Edited and with an introduction by
PHIL COUSINEAU

Photographs by
ERIC LAWTON

RAINCOAST BOOKS

Vancouver

First published in 2000 by
Raincoast Books
8680 Cambie Street
Vancouver, B.C.
v6p 6m9
(604) 323-7100
www.raincoast.com

Interior layout design by MARIANNE STOKKE, anna DESIGN
Cover design by LESLIE SMITH

Canadian Cataloguing in Publication Data
THE SOUL AFLAME
ISBN 1-55192-262-2
Meditations. 2. Devotional calendars.
I. Cousineau, Phil. II. Lawton, Eric.
bl624.2.S678 1999 • 291.4'32 • c99-910491-8

Printed and bound in Singapore

THE CANADA COUNCIL | LE CONSEIL DES ARTS
FOR THE ARTS | DU CANADA
SINCE 1957 | DEPUIS 1957

Raincoast Books gratefully acknowledges the support of the Government of Canada, through the Book Publishing Industry Development Program, the Canada Council for the Arts and the Department of Canadian Heritage. We also acknowledge the assistance of the Province of British Columbia, through the British Columbia Arts Council.

To the memory of my beloved uncle and aunt,
   Cy and Barb McCann,
   whose faith in my fire
   kept alive the fire in my faith,

and to my oldest friend, Steve Shrope,
   with faith in your fire.
                    PHIL COUSINEAU
                    San Francisco, June 1999

For my Father, Leo Lawton,
   Who taught me the potential of wonder,
   and that one should always allow for miracles
   and what it means to love, no matter what.

For my beloved child, Alexandra Rose,
   Who came into this world as my Dad was leaving it,
   and shared with him that most precious of special times
   and received from him the gift of fascination.
                    ERIC LAWTON,
                    Los Angeles, April 1999

Everything we need to know about life
can be found in the fathom-long body.

GAUTAMA SIDDHARTHA BUDDHA

My heart is sad and lonely,
for you I sigh, for you, dear, only.
Why haven't you seen it?
I'm all for you, body and soul.

SARAH VAUGHN

How to spend a day nobly, is the problem to be solved,
beside which all the great reforms which are preached
seem to me trivial. If any day has not the privilege
of an action, then at least raise it by a passion.

RALPH WALDO EMERSON

CONTENT

ACKNOWLEDGMENTS

I wish to express my gratitude to all those surefire souls who helped kindle the flame of this project, especially my coauthor and friend, Eric Lawton, whose remarkable images grace this book, and the master cellist David Darling, with whom we collaborated at the Esalen Institute workshops that inspired these books of hours.

My deep thanks also to our publisher, Kevin Williams, at Raincoast Books, and our editor Brian Scrivener for their faith in the soulful potential of this book, Les Smith and Marianne Stokke for their dedication to its inspirational design, and the irrepressible Brenda Knight of Conari Press who kept the fire stoked.

A bonfire of gratitude also to those whose suggestions helped mightily along the way, especially John Nance, Trish O'Rielly, Alex Eliot, Valerie Andrews, Lawrence Beaton, Chris Donges and Huston Smith, who has embodied for me the graceful way to tend the fire of the soul.

Finally, incandescent thanks to Jo Beaton, my keeper of the flame.

PHIL COUSINEAU

A book such as this could not exist without the contribution of many people. Some helped directly, with ideas, expertise and encouragement. Some will never know how meaningful their momentary glance could be: a fleeting window into a world, an emotion, a familiar, timeless state of the human condition.

From the first group, I would like to thank those caring people who helped me to bring ideas to reality, especially:

Phil Cousineau, my friend and collaborator for these fifteen years. No matter how loud the winds howl in my too frenetic pace, Phil is ever the faithful pilgrim, focused on the seeker's path of the mind and spirit, the journey of the soul. Phil is the alchemist who finds the magic between the words, and turns that quiet space into an experience that all of us can gratefully share.

My Mother, Vira Lawton, whose stories of her childhood in China and Europe set me off on the travels, both outward and inward, that resulted in this book.

My wife, Gail, who took in this errant soul and gave me the greatest gift of all, our family; and our beautiful daughters, Rebecca and Alexandra, who fill me with joy as I watch them learn and grow, and who light my days.

Chayim Frenkel, Andrew Ungerleider, Rand De Mattei and Arthur Secunda, who, each in his own unique way, have helped me along my way in this life of images and ideas.

My dear friends and family, who mean so much to me.

Neil Rubenstein, Rod Ibanez and Travis Eastepp for their skill and craftsmanship.

Kevin Williams, Brian Scrivener and Les Smith at Raincoast Books; Claudia Schaab and Brenda Knight at Conari Press, for their support, perseverence and creativity in bringing this book to life.

From the second group, I thank all those who opened their worlds to me in years of journeys to distant lands, sometimes for just a timeless moment, within whose eyes I found my own.

ERIC LAWTON

INTRODUCTION

"Where Do We Come From? What Are We? Where Are We Going?" These words hover in the upper left hand corner of a painting set in the lush South Pacific by the French artist Paul Gauguin. Timeless questions like these have fired the imagination of human beings from the Paleolithic caves of our most ancient ancestors to the futuristic workshops of the wizards in Silicon Valley. They reveal the way our thoughts turn toward the infinite during the luminous moments of our lives – such as when we gaze with awe into the eyes of our newborn children, caress the brows of loved ones who have died, or wonder how we might live more passionately.

Struck by awe and wonder – or fear and trembling – we grope for a word or image that might describe the spark of life, its secret essence, the strange presence we often feel within ourselves. The need to describe this vital force reveals a deep desire to understand the hidden fire within our very core – then learn how to stoke the embers there.

To do this takes what the ancients called a "genius" for life itself, the spirit for getting the most out of our time and the courage to make the transition between numbly going through the motions of our lives – to living with our whole heart and soul. Our days demand fire, as Emerson said, and all the powers that we can summon. But the demands of everyday life make it difficult to stay impassioned for long.

The Irish poet Susan L. Mitchell reflected on the fleeting nature of the inspired life:

The breath that blows
The soul aflame is still a wandering wind
That comes and goes

In the sublime mythology of the soul's descent into the body breath kindles life. Something from the back of beyond *breathes* into us, say poets, mystics and sages of many traditions. First there was nothing – then there was something: *life*. Nothing – then the moment of *quickening* – then nothing again? Throughout our life our vitality comes and goes. So it is no coincidence to discover notions of soul and wind or breath connected the world over. For as breath comes and goes so does life itself.

Our own English word for soul has its roots in *sawal*, the Anglo-Saxon word for breath. Similarly, *psyche* and *pneuma* in Greek, *anima* and *spiritus* in Latin, *nephesh* and *ruah* in Hebrew, *prana* in Sanskrit, *qi* in Chinese, all refer to the notion of a force that enlivens us.

Where the soul finally resides is an age-old question. Many tribal cultures, such as the Aztecs and Mayans, believed the vital spark was in the blood. Others, such as the Dayaks of Borneo and the ancient Celts, regarded soul as being in the head. The ancient Egyptians thought soul lay in the tongue, acting as the rudder for the body. The classical Greeks considered soul to hover in the joints of the body. Still other cultures placed soul in the spinal marrow, seminal fluid, brain, hair and nails.

Most familiar is the association of the soul with the heart. The alchemists declared its seat was in the heart. Generations of troubadours and balladeers celebrated its presence there.

The centuries blaze with igneous images for this first principle. The "god-spark," is how the German theologian Meister Eckhardt described the soul. Hildegard von Bingen envisioned a "supreme fiery spark." Paracelsus imagined a "blue flame" and Nikos Kazantzakis a "bird of fire." Philosopher Rudolf Steiner imagined a sunburst, Wassily Kandinsky painted a red triangle, while filmmaker Ingmar Bergman dreamed of "a shadowy red dragon." And what image did the Greeks use to illustrate the "awakening" of Eros, the god of love, but hot wax from the burning candle of Psyche, the love-struck soul.

Warming ourselves beside the fire of these images we find that flame – "the subtlest part of fire" – is a powerful metaphor for soul. A flame gives warmth and light. It forms and shapes, is both palpable and ineffable. It flickers and flares, lunges and leaps, singes and scars, purifies and maintains life, and awakens love in the slumbering heart.

Breath and vitality, fire and flame, body and spirit, soul and inspiration.

These words give us valuable hints about moving between the tranquilized and the invigorated life. The trick is learning how to bring all the elements together. As the old Persian proverb goes, "There are only three kinds of persons in the world: the immovable, the movable, and those that move."

In this spirit, the beat philosopher Alan Watts compared the human condition to a spark plug. For an engine to start, he said, something must leap across the gap in the plug. In people, the void might have been wedged open from a sense of meaninglessness, a lacklove life, a bout of loneliness or sheer anxiety. Whatever the reason, a spark is required if there is to be combustion in the engine of life.

Leaping across the gap of understanding about self-reliance and the vital soul, Emerson elegantly compressed the mystery for his friend John Foster when he said, "Genius is the power for lighting your own flame."

For millennia one of the most burning questions for humanity has been what happens to this mysterious *presence* in us after death. Many scholars, such as Mircea Eliade, believed that speculation about immortality is what first gave rise to the notion of a soul. Where does it go when the breath stops and the heart halts? Where does it hover during a dream? Out of millions of others how does it find its kindred soul in love?

Yet the modern era is marked by a tremendous ambivalence about its very existence, a sensibility captured by Ambrose Bierce's notorious definition of soul as "A spiritual entity about which there hath been brave disputation." The argument ranges from Descartes's exile of the soul to the pineal gland to the recent "astonishing hypothesis" that reduces the mystery of the inward life to chance surges of chemistry in the body. Genuine wonder about an "immortal" soul has transmogrified into anxiety about how the "mortal" soul can survive the pressures of the here-and-now. Since the Industrial Revolution the juggernaut of material progress has paradoxically created what the existentialists called the "anxiety of nothingness." The awesome inward presence that has carried echoes of the divine for centuries has diminished into a mere "ghost in the machine," a disembodied consciousness represented in movies and literature as something drone-like taking over our minds. Beside the fear that computers are becoming more like people is the strange dread that people are becoming more like robots.

But the denial of our inward life only intensifies, at times even literalizes the quest for evidence of the soul. Witness the Great Soul Trial of 1972. The case was precipitated by the disappearance of an eccentric gold miner, James Kidd, who had left his motel room in Phoenix, Arizona, twenty years earlier, to wander into the Superstition Mountains and presumably work his claim. He never returned.

His legal will was discovered in the late 1960s in a bank vault. It stipulated in tortured but earnest syntax that his entire estate (at the time some $16,000) should "go in a research or some scientific proof of a soul of the human body which leaves at death I think their [*sic*] can be a Photograph of soul leaving the human at death."

Five years, a hundred and forty claims by self-proclaimed experts, later, the court awarded Kidd's estate (by this time worth $264,000) to three parapsychology groups who studied out-of-body and near-death experiences. Their findings were interesting but inconclusive. Their report was derisively dismissed in the obituary pages of the *New York Times* on June 16, 1975, with the headline, "Researchers Aided by Hermit's Will Fail to Find a Soul."

The poor gold miner's legacy is bittersweet. His soul-searching is touching, but also indicative of the savage doubt about the authenticity of our own inward lives. But the soul does not need physical evidence anymore than lovers need authentication from chemists that the cascading of phenylethylamine through our hearts "proves" the existence of their love. Nor do friends need the verification that friendship is a 'positive feedback loop in our circuitry' – as Data the droid in *Star Trek: The Next Generation* coolly described it.

But the stuff of soul cannot be detected as an ethereal substance somewhere in the body that might pop up in a photograph or be silhouetted on an x-ray or tracked on an encephelogram. As Albert Einstein himself said, "Body and soul are not two separate things, but only two ways of perceiving the same thing." In the inimitable words of Oscar Wilde, "Those who say the body and soul are different have neither."

Anthropologist Barbara Sproul makes a brilliant distinction when she writes,

> *Having misunderstood soul in this fashion (just as we often misunderstand God) we become disappointed when we cannot find it and dismiss it as an illusion, another fraud perpetrated by religion. But soul is not a thing; it is a dimension of depth in a thing. Like justness in a judge's decision, or beauty in a painting, soul is a quality of absoluteness in something relative . . . understood profoundly, people are connected to the holiness of the world in such a way that they reveal a dimension of holiness in themselves, a dimension of depth that is absolute.*

The sacred energies that smolder in us are a "throng of invisibles," as psychologist James Hillman refers to them – powers that reveal themselves in our experience of the depth dimension, the holiness of the world. To experience them we need a capacious imagination, intense commitment to living as creatively as possible, and deep attention to the inner qualities of our lives.

The true search is for "the necessary fire," as John Gardner advised Raymond Carver about the writing life. We need to believe, as Carver did when he was racked with doubt about his talent, that the fire is there, that a creative force exists that can be harnessed, and that we, like Beckett in his fabled last lines of *Krapp's Last Tapes,* cannot give up, "not with the fire in me now."

That depth defies measurement. What is required is personal experience, as revealed by the poet Emily Dickinson, who could write with deep conviction, "I cannot see my soul, but know 'tis there."

It is there in sudden raptured moments, such as the fiery embrace of love, fathoms-deep dream journeys, the grip of near-death encounters or throes of religious revelation, the creative flames of inspiration. As the religious historian Huston Smith writes, we sense the soul "indelibly in the incommunicable sense of what it feels like to be oneself instead of anyone else who has ever lived . . . ." For the Eskimo shaman Intinilik the soul's powers are what "makes us human."

These are large words, ones that strike a deep chord in an age of anxiety about the very possibility of ever knowing our own depths. What all the wisdom traditions agree upon is that we need to tend our own fires through ritual contemplation and creative acts. Without that attention to the inner forces we can never realize the spiritual meaning of our experience. The danger of ignoring them was announced by the Indian poet Kabir seven centuries ago when he wrote, "If you can't find where your soul is, for you the world will never be real."

The ancient Greeks had some sage advice for this dilemma, in their legendary Delphic wisdom: "The soul, to know itself, must gaze upon another soul."

For this degree of luminosity it helps to have a splendid prism. For that we turn to the medieval model of *The Book of Hours.*

Long have we tried to read eternity into the world, but rarely has the story of the pilgrimage of the soul been rendered as remarkably as it was in medieval Europe. During the traumatic upheaval of the late Middle Ages, the rise of the middle class, increasing literacy and widening prosperity made possible a revolution in bookmaking. Beyond the musty *scriptoria* of the clergy, more books were produced than at any time since classical antiquity. And none was more prized than the gloriously illuminated manuscript called *The Book of Hours.* For the next two hundred and fifty years, these lavish Latin prayer books were the most popular books of the day, medieval best-sellers intended not for the clergy but for ordinary women and men.

The Book of Hours derived from the *Hours of the Virgin,* a passel of devotional prayers and paintings to the Virgin Mary that were offered according to the canonical hours. In this time before time had been mechanized, medieval life revolved around the Church's canonical hours of the day: *Matins* (midnight), *Lauds* (sunrise), *Prime* (6:00 A.M.), *Terce* (9:00 A.M.), *Sext* (noon), *None* (3:00 P.M.), *Vespers* (sunset) and *Compline* (9:00 P.M.). By ritualizing private meditation, the Book of Hours helped laypeople focus on what was sacred about the hours of their own everyday life. Gazing upon iconic images became a form of devotion, reading inspired words was like listening to Gregorian chant. With image and word put together in the miracle of a simplified prayer book you could have a perpetual conversation with the Virgin, the saints – or God.

What cathedrals are to architecture and the "Ave Maria" is to music, the Book of Hours is to literature and painting. Often described as a "cathedral in the palm of the hand," the Book of Hours offers a myriad of stained-glass window views into the medieval world, both cultural and religious. Through this proscenium, the divine mystery of the soul's relationship with God and the divine could be visualized, and by the holy act of naming the hours and the ritual contemplation of their own often personally selected prayers and pictures, secular time was sanctified for ordinary people as it had long been for the privileged few in the cloistered monasteries. The democratization of religion had begun.

The German Romantic poet Novalis once wrote, "The seat of the soul is where the inner and the outer world meet." That insight was one of the guiding inspirations for our first modern book of hours, the "pocket cathedral" that photographer Eric Lawton and I created in 1993, *The Soul of the World.* That book featured fifty-six passages of sacred literature and photographs from fifty-six sacred sites from around the world which evoked what the ancients used to call the *genius loci,* the *anima mundi* – what we call the spirit of place. The idea was to offer a meditative tool that might help modern readers contemplate the beauty of time as well as the beauty of nature. The template of a Book of Hours was in recognition of the accelerated pace that has overtaken modern life, in that its ritualized attention to the hours of the day inspire a simple but elegant way to savor what Thoreau called "the bloom of each moment."

In this companion volume, *The Soul Aflame,* we turn to the inner landscape, as revealed by poets, mystics, explorers, filmmakers, musicians, dancers, scientists, naturalists, cooks and artists who reflect on the soul's thirst for the creative life.

All my life I have been fascinated by the stirring of the imagination. I have found tremendous inspiration in the great wisdom traditions of the world: parables that praise the courageous heart; trickster tales about the ambiguous nature of creativity; poetry that flashes like lightning across the prairie sky; movies that dilate my heart as well as my eyes. These words and images send a *frisson,* the shiver of truth, through me.

The reflections in this book come from thousands of entries I have assiduously copied into my journals over the last twenty-five years. The words here have been meteor showers of inspiration for me. I have used them whenever I have needed to ignite a new project, or simply needed the shudder of truth to get me through my own dark nights of doubt.

I have chosen passages that praise the fabled embrace of Eros and Psyche, of body and soul, while Eric has selected photographs that best "sing the body electric," in the ecstatic phrasing of Walt Whitman. To accomplish this demands the ability to see the sacred, an exercise that Eric has practiced whole-heartedly in his world travels. Over and over again he has found what Stieglitz called "equivalents" for the soul's mood. His passionate eye has helped people around the world experience what is holy about the natural world and noble about the human adventure.

Our current collaboration seeks an alternative vision to what Susan Griffin calls the modern tragedy of "disembodied spiritual existence." Devoid of reverence for the link of body and soul it is difficult to viscerally feel the spark of inspiration. So, together in word and image, we are not attempting to capture the literal soul springing from the body, but rather to fathom the mysterious moments when the body expresses the divine fire – in the eyes, the face, the gestures, the movements, the stillness. As Leonardo da Vinci wrote, "If anyone wishes to see how the soul dwells in its body, let him observe how this body uses its daily habitation."

As in traveling to remote places and seeing what is universal in human nature, to contemplate (which originally meant to build a temple within the body) the soulful moments of others can help lead us back to our own wayward souls.

To do that takes courage and fire and a leap of faith, which is to say it takes love.

For love is the spark that leaps the gap in every life. "Love is himself so divine a poet," as Plato wrote, "that he can kindle in the souls of others the poetic fire, for no matter what dull clay we seemed to be before, we are every one of us a poet when we are in love."

In this way love is the elusive spark in the tinderbox of the soul that sets the soul aflame. Love for our families, our work, our community. Love of the body's treasures, as Mirabai declares here; the work we devote ourselves to, as Van Gogh confesses; the arrival of our beloved, as we hear from Christina Rossetti; the moment when "of a sudden" our bodies blaze with happiness, as we read in Yeats.

Every time we feel that slow combustion inside ourselves, we discover fire as if for the first time. The fire glows there in the way we live and love and learn. Slowly, the world becomes more real each time we discover the flame at the heart of our every hour of the day. If we make the conscious choice to squeeze the bellows of our imagination, the flame *lives*.

The soul is a flame, wrote Nikos Kazantzakis, "a bird of fire that leaps from bough to bough, from head to head, and that shouts: 'I cannot stand still, I cannot be consumed, no one can quench me.'"

What we feel most deeply leads us to the lost kingdom of the imagination. That is where we will find the genius of love, the stirred heart, the spark of joy, the flare of the charged imagination, the incandescence of the creative life, the heat from the soul aflame.

PHIL COUSINEAU
North Beach, San Francisco, California

.

SUNDAY

My soul is a furnace happy with the fire.

MEVLANA RUMI

MATINS

O friend, understand: the body
is like the ocean,
rich with hidden treasures.

Open your inmost chamber and light its lamp.

Within the body are gardens,
rare flowers, peacocks, the inner Music;
within the body a lake of bliss,
on it the white soul-swans take their joy.

And in the body, a vast market –
go there, trade,
sell yourself for a profit you can't spend.

Mira says, her Lord is beyond praising.
Allow her to dwell near Your feet.

MIRABAI,
Indian(1498-1565?),
translated by Jane Hirshfield

Mandalay, Burma

LAUDS

Our birth is but a sleep and a forgetting;
The Soul that riseth with us, our life's Star,
Hath had elsewhere its setting,
And rises from afar.
Not in entire forgetfulness,
And not in utter nakedness,
But trailing clouds of glory do we come
From God, who is our home:
Heaven lies about us in our infancy! . . .

O joy! that in our embers
Is something that doth live,
That nature yet remembers
What was so fugitive! . . .

Hence in a season of calm weather
Though inland far we be
Our souls have sight of that immortal sea
Which brought us hither,
Can in a moment travel thither,
And see the children sport upon the shore,
And hear the mighty waters rolling evermore.

WILLIAM WORDSWORTH,
English (1770-1850)

Imperial Palace, Beijing, China

PRIME

Love is apart from all things.
Desire and excitement are nothing beside it.
It is not the body that finds love.
What leads us there is the body.
What is not love provokes it.
What is not love quenches it.
Love lays hold of everything we know.
The passions which are called love
also change everything to a newness
at first. Passion is clearly the path
but does not bring us to love.
It opens the castle of our spirit
so that we might find the love which is
a mystery hidden there.
Love is one of many great fires.
Passion is a fire made of many woods,
each of which gives off its special odor
so we can know the many kinds
that are not love. Passion is the paper
and twigs that kindle the flames
but cannot sustain them. Desire perishes
because it tries to be love.
Love is eaten away by appetite.
Love does not last, but it is different
from the passions that do not last.
Love lasts by not lasting.
Isaiah said each man walks in his own fire
for his sins. Love allows us to walk
in the sweet music of our particular heart.

JACK GILBERT,
American

Santa Monica, California

TERCE

When I think of you,
fireflies in the marsh rise
like the soul's jewels,
lost to eternal longing
abandoning my body.

> Izumi Shikibu,
> *Japanese (970-1030),*
> *translated by Sam Hamill*

White moth, flutter off:
Fly back into
My breast now
Quickly, my own soul!

> Wafu,
> *Japanese (18th century),*
> *unknown translator*

Kathmandu, Nepal

SEXT

Age cannot reach me where the veils of God have shut me in,
For me the myriad births of stars and suns do but begin,
And here how fragrantly there blows to me the holy breath,
Sweet from the flowers and stars and hearts of men,
    From life and death.

We are not old, O heart, we are not old,
    The breath that blows
The soul aflame is still a wandering wind
    That comes and goes;
And the stirred heart with sudden raptured life a moment
    glows.

A moment here – a bulrush's brown head in the gray rain,
A moment there – a child drowned and a heart quickened with
    pain;
The name of Death, the blue deep heaven, the scent of the salt
    sea,
The spicy grass, the honey robbed from the wild bee.

Awhile we walk the world on its wide roads and narrow ways,
And they pass by, the countless shadowy troops of nights and
    days;
We know them not, O happy heart, for you and I
Watch where within a slow dawn lightens up another sky.

      Susan L. Mitchell,
      Irish (1868-1930)

Bhaktapur, Nepal

NONE

My fiftieth year had come and gone,
I sat, a solitary man,
In a crowded London shop,
An open book and empty cup
On the marble table-top.

While on the shop and street I gazed
My body of a sudden blazed;
And twenty minutes more or less
It seemed, so great my happiness,
That I was blesséd and could bless.

WILLIAM BUTLER YEATS,
Irish (1856-1939)

Bahamas

VESPERS

In my opinion I am often as rich as Croesus, not in money,
but rich because I have found in my work something to
which I can devote myself with heart and soul, and which
gives inspiration and zest to life. Of course my moods vary,
but I have a certain average serenity. I have a certain *faith* in
art, a certain confidence, which is a powerful stream that
drifts a man into harbor, though he must do his bit, too.
I may be in comparatively great difficulties, and there are
gloomy days in my life, but I think it such a great blessing
when a man found his work that I cannot myself [find] the
courage to undertake it, the expenses are so great, beginning
with a model and food and housing and ending with colors
and brushes – and that is also like a weaving-loom where
the different threads must be kept apart. But I am privileged
above many others.

> VINCENT VAN GOGH,
> *Dutch (1853-1890)*

Tibetan refugee camp, near Pokhara, Nepal

COMPLINE

But there is something that I must say to my people who stand on the warm threshold which leads to the palace of justice. In the process of gaining our rightful place we must not be guilty of wrongful deeds. Let us not seek to satisfy our thirst for freedom by drinking from the cup of bitterness and hatred. We must forever conduct our struggle on the high plane of dignity and discipline. We must not allow our creative protest to degenerate into physical violence. Again and again we must rise to the majestic heights of meeting physical force with soul force.

MARTIN LUTHER KING, JR.,
African-American (1929-1968)

near Loeyangalani, Lake Turkana, Kenya

MONDAY

Man has no Body distinct from his Soul;
for that called Body is a portion of soul
discern'd by the Five Senses, the chief inlets
of Soul in this age.

WILLIAM BLAKE

MATINS

Lord, my mind is not noisy with desires,
  and my heart has satisfied its longing.
I do not care about religions
  or anything that is not you.
I have soothed and quieted my soul,
  like a child at its mother's breast.
My soul is as peaceful as a child
  sleeping in its mother's arms.

  Psalm 131,
  translated by Stephen Mitchell

The woman is the fire,
her womb the fuel,
the invitations of man, the smoke.
The door is the flame,
entering the ember,
pleasure the spark.
In this fire gods form the offering.
From this offering springs the child.

  from the Chandogya Upanishads,
  translated by A. B. Keith

near Yangshuo, China

LAUDS

I don't want to be the only one here
Telling all the secrets –

Filling up all the bowls at this party,
Taking all the laughs.

I would like you
To start putting things on the table
That can also feed the soul
The way I do.
That way
We can invite
A hell of a lot more
Friends.

SHAMS-UD-DIN MUHAMMAD HAFIZ,
Persian (c. 1320-1389),
version by Daniel Landinsky

Tahiti

PRIME

I said to myself, – I said to others, –
"There comes into my mind such an indescribable, infinite,
all-absorbing, divine, heavenly pleasure, a sense of elevation
and expansion, and [I] have had nought to do with it. I perceive
that I am dealt with by superior powers. This is a pleasure, a
joy, an existence which I have not procured myself. I speak as
a witness on the stand, and tell what I have perceived." The
morning and the evening were sweet to me, and I led a life
aloof from society of men. I wondered if a mortal had ever
known what I knew. I looked in books for some recognition of
a kindred experience, but, strange to say, I found none. Indeed,
I was slow to discover that other men had had this experience,
for it had been possible to read books and to associate with
men on other grounds. The maker of me was improving me.
When I detected this interference I was profoundly moved.
For years I marched as to a music in comparison with which
the military music of the streets is noise and discord. I was
daily intoxicated, and yet no man could call [me] intemperate.
With all your science can you tell how it is, and whence it is,
that light comes into the soul?

> HENRY DAVID THOREAU,
> *American (1817-1862),*
> *Journal, July 16, 1851*

outside Elsinore Castle, Denmark

TERCE

All night I could not sleep
Because of the moonlight on my bed.
I kept on hearing a voice calling:
Out of Nowhere, Nothing answered, "yes."

> ZI YE (TZU YEH),
> *Chinese (6th-3rd century B.C.E.),*
> *translated by Arthur Waley*

After the final no there comes a yes,
And on that yes the future world depends.

> WALLACE STEVENS,
> *American (1879 –1955)*

. . . and then he asked me would I yes to say yes my
mountain flower and first I put my arms around him yes
and drew him down to me so he could feel my breasts all
perfume yes and his heart was going like mad and yes I
said yes I will Yes.

> JAMES JOYCE,
> *Irish (1882-1941)*

Oaxaca, Mexico

SEXT

When the great Rabbi Israel Baal Shem-Tov saw misfortune
threatening the Jews it was his custom to go into a certain part
of the forest to meditate. There he would light a fire, say a
special prayer, and the miracle would be accomplished and the
misfortune averted. Later, when his disciple, the celebrated
Magid of Mezritch, had occasion, for the same reason, to
intercede with heaven, he would go to the same place in the
forest and say: "Master of the Universe, listen! I do not know
how to light the fire, but I am still able to say the prayer," and
again the miracle would be accomplished. Still later, Rabbi
Moshe-Leib of Sasov, in order to save his people once more,
would go into the forest and say: "I do not know how to light
the fire, I do not know the prayer, but I know the place and
this must be sufficient." It was sufficient and the miracle
was accomplished. Then it fell to Rabbi Israel of Rizhyn to
overcome misfortune. Sitting in his armchair, his head in his
hands, he spoke to God: "I am unable to light the fire and I do
not know the prayer; I cannot even find the place in the forest.
All I can do is to tell the story, and this must be sufficient."
And it was sufficient. God made man because he loves stories.

ELIE WIESEL,
American

Old City, Jerusalem, Israel

NONE

I am the poet of the Body and I am the poet of the Soul,
The pleasures of heaven are with me and the pains of hell are with me,
The first I graft and increase upon myself, the latter I translate into a
   new tongue.

I am the poet of the woman the same as the man,
And I say it is great to be a woman as to be a man,
And I say there is nothing greater than the mother of men . . .

I have said that the soul is not more than the body,
And I have said that the body is not more than the soul,
And nothing, not God, is greater to one than one's self is . . .

And I say to any man or woman, Let your soul stand cool
   and composed before a million universes . . .

O my body! I dare not desert the likes of you in other men
   and women, nor the likes of parts of you,
I believe the parts of you are to stand or fall with the likes
   of the soul (and that they are the soul)
I believe that the likes of you shall stand or fall with my poems,
   and that they are my poems . . .

O I say these are not the parts and poems of the body only,
   but of the soul,
O I say now these are the soul!

WALT WHITMAN,
American (1819-1892)

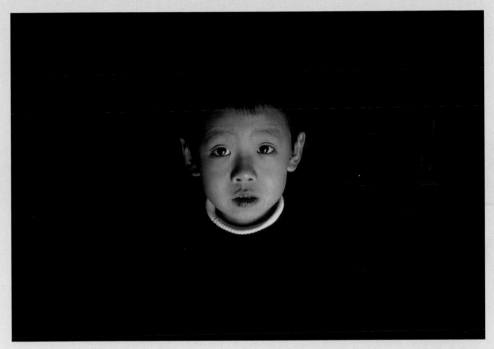

Tienjin, China

VESPERS

There is a vitality, a life force, a quickening that is translated through you into action, and because there is only one of you in all time, this expression is unique.

And if you block it, it will never exist through any other medium and be lost. The world will not have it. It is not your business to determine how good it is:
nor how valuable it is: nor how it compares with other expressions. It is your business to keep it yours clearly and directly, to keep the channel open.

You do not even have to believe in yourself or your work. You have to keep open and aware directly to the urges that motivate YOU.
Keep the channel open . . .

No artist is pleased . . .
There is no satisfaction whatever at any time.
There is only a queer, divine dissatisfaction, a blessed unrest that keeps us marching and makes us more alive than the others.

MARTHA GRAHAM,
American (1884-1991)

Tokyo, Japan

COMPLINE

Invite the Sacred to participate in your joy in little things,
as well as in your agony over the great ones. There are
as many miracles to be seen through a microscope as
through a telescope. Start with the little things seen
through the magnifying glass of wonder, and just as a
magnifying glass can focus the sunlight into a burning
beam that can set a leaf aflame, so can your focused
wonder set you ablaze with insight. Find the light in
each other and just fan it.

ALICE O. HOWELL,
American

Some things lead into the realm beyond words . . .
it is like that small mirror in fairy tales –
you glance in it and what you see is not yourself;
for an instant you glimpse the Inaccessible . . .
and the soul cries out for it.

ALEXANDER SOLZHENITSYN,
Russian

Thimpu, Bhutan

TUESDAY

It's not the earthquake

That controls the advent of a different life

But storms of generosity

And visions of incandescent souls.

Boris Pasternak

MATINS

A very long time ago there was a traveler who was making a journey across the wild steppes when he suddenly heard the roar of a tiger. Terrified, he turned and saw the beast charging him. The traveler wasted no time. He ran for his life across the barren land – but saw no refuge until a dried-up well loomed in the distance. He felt his blood surging as he gripped the edge of the well and leapt inside.

The traveler fell, and as he fell he noticed to his horror a fire-snorting dragon far below, its jaws snapping viciously. Desperately, the traveler reached out and grabbed hold of a long vine growing out of the bricks in the well. Miraculously, the vine held him and for a few precious moments he clung for his life against the cold brick walls of the well.

Above him, the tiger gnashed its teeth. Below him, the dragon licked its chops. The poor traveler's arms grew weary. His thoughts knotted. Fate was very near. Still, he held on. Hope flickered in his heart.

While he pondered his strange dilemma he noticed two mice, one black, one white, nibbling at the branch to which he was clinging. The sight put him into a rapture. Every molecule of bark on the branch glowed as if on fire. It was then he noticed a few drops of luscious honey glistening on the leaves at the root of the vine.

Smiling, he stretched out his tongue and tasted the honey.

Adapted from an old Eastern parable
by Phil Cousineau

Big Bear, California

LAUDS

I think over again my small adventures,
My fears,
Those small ones that seemed so big,
For all the vital things
I had to get and to reach;
And yet there is only one great thing,
The only thing,
To live to see the great day that dawns
And the light that fills the world.

Anonymous,
19th century

Paris, France

PRIME

The soul, like the moon,
is new, and always new again.

And I have seen the ocean
continuously creating.

Since I scoured my mind
and my body, I too, Lalla,
am new, each moment new.

My teacher told me one thing,
Live in the soul.

When that was so,
I began to go naked,
and dance.

> LALLA (LAD DED),
> *Kashmiri (14th century?),*
> *translated by Coleman Barks*

Enchey Monastery, Gangtok, Sikkim

TERCE

Songs are thoughts which are sung out with the
breath when people let themselves be moved by a
great force, and ordinary speech no longer suffices.
A person is moved like an ice-floe which drifts with
the current. His thoughts are driven by a flowing
force when he feels joy, when he feels fear, when he
feels sorrow. Thoughts can surge in on him, causing
him to gasp for breath, and making his heart beat
faster. Something like a softening of the weather will
keep him thawed. And then it will happen that we,
who always think of ourselves as small, will feel even
smaller. And we will hesitate before using words.
But it will happen that the words that we need
will come of themselves –
When the words that we need shoot up of
themselves – we have a new song.

> Orpingalik,
> *Netsilik Inuit (early 20th century),*
> *translated by Tom Lowenstein*

Temple of Heaven, Forbidden City, Beijing, China

SEXT

My heart is like a singing bird
Whose nest is in a watered shoot:
My heart is like an apple-tree
Whose boughs are bent with thickset fruit;
My heart is like a rainbow shell
That paddles in a halcyon sea;
My heart is gladder than all these
Because my love is come to me.

Raise me a dais of silk and down;
Hang it with vair and purple dyes;
Carve it in doves and pomegranates,
And peacocks with a hundred eyes;
Work it in gold silver grapes,
In leaves and silver fleur-de-lys;
Because the birthday of my life
Is come, my love is come to me.

18 November 1857

CHRISTINA ROSSETTI,
English (1830-1894)

Guanajuato, Mexico

NONE

A maiden wept and, as a comforter,
Came one who cried, "I love thee," and he seized
Her in his arms and kissed her with hot breath,
That dried tears upon her flaming cheeks.
While evermore his boldly blazing eye
Burned into hers; but she uncomforted
Shrank from his arms and only wept the more.

Then one came and gazed mutely in her face
With wide and wistful eyes; but still aloof
He held himself; as with a reverent fear,
As one who knows some sacred presence nigh.
And as she wept he mingled tear with tear,
That cheered her soul like dew on a dusty flower, –
Until she smiled, approached, and touched his hand!

PAUL DUNBAR,
African-American (1872-1906)

Thimpu, Bhutan

VESPERS

The most beautiful and most profound emotion we can experience is the sensation of the mystical. It is the sower of all true science. He to whom this emotion is a stranger, who can no longer wonder and stand rapt in awe, is as good as dead. To know what is impenetrable to us really exists, manifesting itself as the highest wisdom and the most radiant beauty which our dull faculties can comprehend only in the most primitive form – this knowledge, this feeling is at the center of true religiousness. The cosmic religious experience is the strongest and oldest mainspring of scientific research. My religion consists of a humble admiration of the illimitable superior spirit who reveals himself in the slight details we are able to perceive with our frail and feeble minds. That deeply emotional conviction of the presence of a superior reasoning power, which is revealed in the incomprehensible universe, forms my idea of God.

ALBERT EINSTEIN,
German-American (1875-1955),
translated by Alan Harris

Kinkakuji Temple, Kyoto, Japan

COMPLINE

I was thrown out of college for cheating on a metaphysical exam.
I looked into the soul of the boy next to me.

WOODY ALLEN,
American

Watching 40 years of my work over the span of one year turned
out to be unexpectedly upsetting, at times unbearable. [The films]
represented the blurred X-rays of my soul. [Cinematography is] a
language that literally is spoken from soul to soul in expressions
that, almost sensuously, escape the restrictive control of the
intellect. In the screenplay [*Cries and Whispers*], I say that I have
thought of the color red as the interior of the soul. When I was a
child, I saw the soul as a shadowy dragon, blue as smoke,
hovering like an enormous winged creature, half bird, half fish.
But inside the dragon everything was red.

INGMAR BERGMAN,
Swedish

Kathmandu, Nepal

WEDNESDAY

The man was walking in the desert,

followed by his companion,

when the Thing swooped down on him.

TEILHARD DE CHARDIN

MATINS

The first peace, which is the most important, is that
which comes within the souls of men when they
realize their relationship, their one-ness, with the
universe and all its powers, and when they realize
that at the center of the universe dwells Wakan-Tanka,
and that this center is really everywhere, it is within
each of us. This is the real peace, and the others are
but reflections of this. The second peace is that which
is made between two individuals, and the third is that
which is made between two nations. But above all you
should understand that there can never be peace
between nations until there is first known that true
peace, which, as I have often said, is within the souls
of men.

> BLACK ELK,
> *Oglala Sioux (1863-1950)*

Sonada Monastery, Darjeeling

LAUDS

My soul is an enchanted boat
Which, like a sleeping swan, doth float
Upon the silver waves of thy sweet singing;
And thine doth like an angel sit
Beside a helm conducting it,
Whilst all the winds with melody are ringing,
It seems to float ever, for ever,
Upon that many-winding river,
Between mountains, woods, abysses,
A paradise of wildernesses!
Till, like one in slumber bound,
Borne to the ocean, I float down, around,
Into a sea profound, of ever-spreading sound . . . .

PERCY BYSSHE SHELLEY,
English (1792-1822)

near Yangshuo, China

PRIME

Exultation is the going
Of an inland soul to sea,
Past the houses – past the headlands –
Into deep Eternity –

Bred as we, among the mountains,
Can the sailor understand
The divine intoxication
Of the first league out from land?

EMILY DICKINSON,
American (1830-1886)

Asilomar, California

TERCE

How wonderful is the human voice! It is indeed the organ of the soul! The intellect of man sits enthroned visibly upon the forehead and in his eye; and the heart of man is written upon his countenance. But the soul reveals itself in the voice only, as God revealed himself to the prophet of old, in "the still, small voice," and in a voice from the burning bush. The soul of man is audible, not visible. A sound alone betrays the flowing of the eternal fountain, invisible to man!

HENRY DAVID LONGFELLOW,
American (1807-1882)

Well, I think soul is certainly a feeling that is transmitted in one way or another. There is a transmitter and there is a receiver. Sometimes the transmitter is the artist, and the receiver is the audience, and sometimes it's vice versa. In those moments of spontaneity, the audience is the transmitter and the artist is the receiver. It's something that's very empathetic – and it's deep. Soul is deep.

ARETHA FRANKLIN,
African-American

Mandalay, Burma

SEXT

Roxane:
Ah, hush!

Cyrano:
A kiss, when all is said, is – what?
A compact sealed, a promise carried out.
An oath accomplished and a vow confirmed.
The rosy dot upon the "i" in "loving."
A secret for no ear, but for the lips.
The velvet humming of an amorous bee:
The endless moment of infinity.
The heart's communion cup that tastes of flowers.
The breathing in a little of the soul
When the pure spirit rises to the lips.

Roxane:
Ah, hush.

from CYRANO DE BERGERAC,
by EDWARD ROSTAND,
French (1868-1918),
translated by Louis Untermeyer

Los Angeles, California

N·O·N·E

One day in Burghölzli, the famous institute in Zurich where the words "schizophrenia" and "complex" were born, I watched a woman being interviewed. She sat in a wheel-chair because she was elderly and feeble. She said that she was dead for she had lost her heart. The psychiatrist asked her to place her hand over her breast to feel her heart beating; it must still be there if there she could feel its beat. "That," she said, "is not my real heart." She and the psychiatrist looked at each other. There was nothing more to say. Like the primitive who has lost his soul, she had lost the loving courageous connection to life – and that is the real heart, not the ticker which can as well pulsate isolated in a glass bottle.

This is a different view of reality from the usual one. It is so radically different that it forms part of the syndrome of insanity. But one can have as much understanding for the woman in her psychotic depersonalization as for the view of reality of the man attempting to convince her that her heart was indeed still there. Despite the elaborate and moneyed systems of medical research and the advertisements of the health and recreation industries to prove that the real is the physical and that loss of heart and loss of soul are only in the mind, I believe the primitive and the woman in the hospital: we can and do lose our souls. I believe with Jung that each of us is a modern man in search of his soul.

JAMES HILLMAN,
American

Huangshan, China

VESPERS

"Hmm," he said. "Lookie, Ma. I been all day an' all
night hidin' alone. Guess who I been thinkin' about?
Casy! He talked a lot. Used ta bother me.
But now I been thinkin' about what he said, an' I can
remember – all of it. Says one time he went out in the
wilderness to find his own soul, an' he foun' he didn'
have no soul that was his'n. Says he foun' he jus' got
a little piece of a great big soul. Says a wilderness
ain't no good, 'cause his little piece of a soul wasn't no
good 'less it was with the rest, an' was whole. Funny
how I remember. Didn' think I was even listenin'.
But I know now a fella ain't no good alone."

In the souls of the people the grapes of wrath
are filling and growing heavy, growing heavy
for the vintage.

> JOHN STEINBECK,
> *American (1902-1969)*

Santa Monica, California

COMPLINE

On the rough wet grass of the back yard my father and mother have spread quilts. We all lie there, my mother, my father, my uncle, my aunt, and I, too, am lying there. First we were sitting up, then one of us lay down, and then we all lay down, on our stomachs, or on our sides, or on our backs, and they have kept on talking. They are not talking much, and the talk is quiet, of nothing in particular, of nothing at all in particular, of nothing at all. The stars are wide and alive, they seem each like a smile of great sweetness, and they seem very near. All my people are larger bodies than mine, quiet, with voices gentle and meaningless like the voices of sleeping birds. One is an artist, he is living at home. One is a musician, she is living at home. One is my mother who is good to me. One is my father who is good to me. By some chance, here they are, all on this earth; and who shall ever tell the sorrow of being on this earth; lying, on quilts, on the grass, in a summer evening among the sounds of the night. May God bless my people, my uncle, my aunt, my mother, my good father, oh, remember them kindly in their time of trouble; and in the hour of their taking away.

After a little I am taken in and put to bed. Sleep, soft smiling, draws me unto her: and those who receive me, who quietly treat me, as one familiar and well-beloved in that home: but will not, oh, will not, not now, not ever; but will not ever tell me who I am.

JAMES AGEE,
American (1909-1955)

Yucatan (near Chichen Itza), Mexico

THURSDAY

I think with my body which effervesces.

Anna Swir

MATINS

By arising in faith and watchfulness,
by self-possession and self-harmony,
the wise man makes an island for his soul,
which many waters cannot overflow.

But those who know the Real is,
and know the unreal is not,
they shall indeed reach the Truth,
safe on the path of right thought.

GAUTAMA SIDDHARTHA BUDDHA,
Indian (563?-483? B.C.E.),
translated by Juan Mascaró

Baidam Lake, Pokhara, Nepal

LAUDS

It was the wind that gave them life.
It is the wind that comes out of our mouths now
that gives us life.
When this ceases to blow we die.
In the skin of our fingers we can see the
trail of the wind;
it shows us where the wind blew when
our ancestors were created.

WASHINGTON MATTHEWS,
American (19th century)

near Yangshuo, China

PRIME

When her doctor took her bandages off and led her into the garden, the girl who was no longer blind saw "the tree with the lights in it." It was for this tree I searched through the peach orchards of summer, in the forests of fall and down winter and spring for years. Then one day I was walking along Tinker Creek thinking of nothing at all and I saw the tree with the lights in it. I saw the backyard cedar where the mourning doves roost charged and transfigured, each cell buzzing with flame. I stood on the grass with the lights in it, grass that was wholly fire, utterly focused and utterly dreamed. It was less like seeing than like being for the first time seen, knocked breathless by a powerful glance. The flood of fire abated, but I'm still spending the power. Gradually the lights went out in the cedar, the colors died, the cells unflamed and disappeared. I was still ringing. I had been my whole life a bell, and never knew it until at that moment I was lifted and struck. I have since only very rarely seen the tree with the lights in it. The vision comes and goes, mostly goes, but I live for it, for the moment when the mountains open and a new light roars in spate through the crack, and the mountains slam.

ANNIE DILLARD,
American

Huangshan, China

TERCE

Whenever I hurt, wherever I tingle, whenever I weep,
whenever I guffaw, my soul is humming . . . .
It operates in my heart, my deep guts, my genitals.
My soul entangles me in fantasies and
surprising emotions.

JAMES BROUGHTON,
American

The soul is one of the most sensitive parts of the
body. You can ask ten people and get ten different
answers. Soul is whatever rings your bell. But soul is
definitely within the body; it's in the mind of the
observer, like plugging a cord into a receptor.

HELEN MAYBELL ANGLIN,
African-American

El Molo Island, Lake Turkana, Kenya

SEXT

Love is the astrolabe of God's secrets.
This way or that, love guides all to eternity.
Words may enable us to understand,
but ineffable love . . . is the best enlightener.
The intellect becomes like a donkey mired
in mud in its efforts to explain love.
It is love which explains love . . .
The evidence of the sun is the sun.
If you require proof, turn your face from it . . . .

MEVLANA RUMI,
Turkish (1207-1273),
translated by Yasar Nuri Ozturk
and Richard Blakney

Los Angeles, California

NONE

Man not only lives on a physical plane,
but also in a world impregnated with
profound and mysterious forces.
These forces flare-up evoking
deep feelings in the heart of man,
and ignite his soul with questions
to which his intuition strives to prove
the answers.
These inquiries flame-up into the
light and bring with them the darkness
before creation.
Man's senses are aroused by these
'Unknowns'.
They challenge his imagination
as though holding the key which
unlocks his secret hopes;
his desires;
his aspirations;
always leading man on in the quest
of knowledge.

IRENE RICE PEREIRA,
American (1902-1971)

Paris, France

VESPERS

I remember something Zorba told me once:

"One night on a snow-covered Macedonian mountain a terrible wind arose. It shook the little hut where I had sheltered and tried to tip it over, But I had shored it up and straightened it. I was sitting alone by the fire, laughing at and taunting the wind. 'You won't get into my little hut, brother! I shan't open the door to you. You won't put my fire out!; you won't tip my hut over!'"

In these few words of Zorba's I had understood how men should behave and what tone they should adopt when addressing powerful but blind necessity. I walked rapidly along the beach, talking with the invisible enemy. I cried: "You won't get into my soul! I shan't open the door to you! You won't put my fire out; you won't tip me over!"

I walked along the edge of the water to say goodbye to this solitary beach, to engrave it upon my mind and carry it away with me. I had known much joy and many pleasures on that beach. My life with Zorba had enlarged my heart; some of his words had calmed my soul. This man with his infallible instinct and his primitive eagle-like look had taken confident short cuts and, without even losing his breath, had reached the peak of effort and had even gone farther.

NIKOS KAZANTZAKIS,
Greek (1883-1957),
translated by Carl Wildman

Bhaktapur, Nepal

COMPLINE

At night, in my dream, I stoutly climbed a mountain,
Going out alone with my staff of holly-wood.
A thousand crags, a hundred hundred valleys –
In my dream-journey none were unexplored
And all the while my feet never grew tired
And my step was as strong as in my young days.
Can it be that when the mind travels backward
The body also returns to its old state?
And can it be, as between body and soul,
That the body may languish, while the soul is
still strong?
Soul and body – both are vanities:
Dreaming and waking – both alike unreal.
In the day my feet are palsied and tottering;
In the night my steps go striding over the hills.
As day and night are divided in equal parts –
Between the two, I *get* as much as I *lose*.

PO CHÜ-I,
Chinese (772-846),
translated by Arthur Waley

Peru

FRIDAY

The soul's answer to the problem of time
is the experience of timeless being.
There is no other answer.

JACOB NEEDLEMAN

MATINS

My body, you are an animal
whose appropriate behavior
is concentration and discipline.
An effort
of an athlete, of a saint and of a yogi.

Well trained
you may become for me
a gate
through which I will leave myself
and a gate
through which I will enter myself.
A plumb line to the center of the earth
and a cosmic ship to Jupiter.

My body, you are an animal
for whom ambition
is right.
Splendid possibilities
are open to us.

ANNA SWIR,
Polish (1909-1984),
translated by Czeslaw Milosz and
Leonard Nathan

Los Angeles, California

LAUDS

So many people gave me something or were
something to me without knowing it . . . .
I always think that we all live, spiritually, by what
others have given us in the significant hours of
our life. These significant hours do not announce
themselves as coming but arrive unexpected.

We find ourselves in a new movement of thought.
In a movement where, through science and
through the searching of our hearts, everything
has become mysterious. Science has led us from
knowledge to knowledge but also from mystery to
mystery. Mystery alone can lead us on to true
spirituality, to accept and be filled with the mystery
of life in our existence.

ALBERT SCHWEITZER,
Alsatian (1875-1965)

Taxco, Mexico

PRIME

So what is it, this force which makes saints, heroes, geniuses, which makes men pursue their destinies to the end? It seems to me that attention is the state of mind which allows us to perceive what has to be. It is a form of the vision experienced by the great mystics, on days when they were granted a profound concentration. I have the impression that the more I try to think of the essentials of music, the more they seem to depend on general human values. It's all very well to be a musician, it's all very well to be a genius, but the intrinsic value which constitutes your mind, your heart, your sensibility, depends on what you are. You may have to lead a life in which no one understands who you are. Nevertheless I believe that everything depends on attention. I only see you if I pay attention. I only exist, in my own eyes, if I pay attention to myself. One always comes back, willy nilly, to the great words. Have you or have you not received grace? Saint Teresa of Avila, afflicted despite everything with arid prayer, has visions; we say to ourselves, "She is mad, it is hysteria." That's very convenient! Was [Yehudi] Menuhin hysterical while playing sublimely a sublime movement of a Brahms sonata? No, he received the power to penetrate a thought which is neither Brahms's nor his, nor mine; a thought floating in the world, above the world, bearing light.

NADIA BOULANGER,
French (1887-1979),
translated by Robyn Marsack

Judean Desert, Israel

TERCE

You can do anything you want to do. What is rare is this actual wanting to do a certain thing: wanting it so much that you are practically blind to all other things, that nothing else will satisfy you. When you, body and soul, wish to make a certain expression and cannot be distracted from this one desire, then you will be able to make a great use of whatever technical knowledge you have. You will have a clairvoyance, you will see the use of the technique you already have, and you will invent more.

I know I have said a lot when I say "You can do anything you want to do." But I mean it. There is reason for you to give this statement some of your best thought. You may find that this is just what is the matter with most of the people of the world; that few are really wanting what they think they want, and that most people go through their lives without ever doing one whole thing they really want to do.

An artist has got to get acquainted with himself just as much as he can. It is no easy job, for it is not a present-day habit of humanity. This is what I call self-development, self-education. No matter how fine a school you are in, you have to educate yourself . . . .

Blunder ahead with your personal view . . . .
The real work of art is the result of a magnificent struggle.

> Robert Henri,
> *French-American (d. 1929)*

San Francisco, California

SEXT

A aged man is but a paltry thing,
A tattered coat upon a stick, unless
Soul clap its hands and sing, and louder sing
For every tatter in its mortal dress . . . .

> WILLIAM BUTLER YEATS,
> *Irish (1856-1939)*

In the great night my heart will go out;
Toward me the darkness comes rustling.
In the great night my heart will go out.

> OLD PAPAGO WOMAN,
> *translated by Frances Densmore*

Central Taiwan, Republic of China

NONE

To me, animals have all the traits indicative of soul. For soul is not something we can see or measure. We can only observe its outward manifestations: in tears and laughter, in courage and heroism, in generosity and forgiveness. Soul is what's behind-the-scenes in the tough and tender moments when we are most intensely and grippingly alive. But what exactly is soul? Soul is the point at which our lives intersect the timeless, in our love of goodness, our zest for beauty, our passion for truth. Soul is what makes each of our lives a microcosm – not just a meaningless fragment of the universe, but at some level a reflection of the whole.

No one can prove animals have souls. But if we open our hearts to other creatures and allow ourselves to sympathize with their joys and struggles, we find they have the power to touch and transform us. There is an inwardness in other creatures that awakens what is innermost in ourselves.

For ages people have known that animals have a balance and harmony we can learn from. "Ask the beasts, and they will teach you," counsels the Book of Job.

Can we open our hearts to the animals? Can we greet them as our soul mates, beings like ourselves who possess dignity and depth? To do so, we must learn to revere and respect the creatures who, like us, are a part of God's beloved creation, and to cherish the amazing planet that sustains our mutual existence. We must join in a biospirituality that will acknowledge and celebrate the sacred in all life.

GARY KOWALSKI,
American

near Jebel Musa, Sinai Desert

VESPERS

Honor the highest thing in the Universe; it is the power on which all
things depend; it is the light by which all of life is guided. Honor the
highest within yourself; for it, too, is the power on which all things
depend, and the light by which all life is guided. Dig within. Within is
the wellspring of Good; and it is always ready to bubble up, if you just
dig. You have seen a hand, a foot, or perhaps a head severed from its
body and lying some distance away. Such is the state a man brings
himself to – as far as he is able – when he refuses to accept what
befalls him, breaks away from helping others, or pursues self-seeking
action. You become an outcast from the unity of Nature; though born of
it, your own hand has cut you from it. Yet here is the beautiful proviso:
it lies within your own power to join Nature once again. God has not
granted such a favor to any other part of creation: to return again, after
having been separated and cleft asunder. O Universe, all that is in tune
with you is also in tune with me! Every note of your harmony resonates
in my innermost being. For me nothing is early and nothing is late, if it
is timely for you. O Nature, all that your seasons bring is fruit for me.
From thee come all things; in thee do all things live and grow; and to
thee do all things return . . . .
Waste no more time talking about great souls and how they should be.
Become one yourself!

> MARCUS AURELIUS,
> *Roman (121-180),*
> *translated by Maxwell Staniforth*

Taman Negara Jungle, Malaysia

COMPLINE

Eros, blind Father, let me show you the way . . . .
I beg of your all-powerful hands
his sublime body poured in flame
over my body fainted in roses!

The electric corolla I unfold today
offers the nectary of a garden of wives;
in my flesh I surrender to his birds of prey
a whole swarm of rose-colored doves.

Give the two cruel serpents of his embrace,
my tall feverish stalk . . . .Honey, absinthe,
pour on me from his mouth, from his veins . . . .

Lying here before him, I am a burning furrow
that can nourish the seed
of another Breed sublimely insane!

> DELMIRA AGUSTINI,
> *Uruguayan (1887-1914),*
> *translated by Perry Higman*

Siliguri, India

SATURDAY

The inner fire is the most important thing
mankind possesses.

EDITH SÖDERGRAN

MATINS

I am the wind which breathes upon the sea,
I am the wave of the ocean,
I am the murmur of the billows,
I am the ox of the seven combats,
I am the vulture upon the rocks,
I am a beam of the sun,
I am the fairest of plants,
I am a wild boar in valor,
I am a salmon in the water,
I am a lake in the plain,
I am a word of science,
I am the point of the lance of battle,
I am the God who created in the head the fire.
Who is it who throws light into the meeting on the mountain?
Who announces the ages of the moon?
Who teaches the place where couches the sun?
(If not I)

AMERGIN *(attributed),*
Irish (5th-6th century),
translated by Douglas Hyde

near Madurai, Southern India

LAUDS

You must concentrate upon and concentrate
yourself wholly to each day, as though a fire
were raging in your hair.

DESHIMARU,
Zen master (unknown dates)

The heart of men has been so made by God that,
like a flint, it contains a hidden fire which is evolved
by music and harmony, and renders man beside
himself with ecstasy. These harmonies are echoes
of that higher world of reality which we call the
world of spirits . . . . they fan into a flame whatever
love is already dormant in the heart.

AL-GHAZZALI,
Arabic (12th century)

God is a fire in the head.

NIJINSKY,
Russian (1890-1950)

India

PRIME

For the will is like a fire, baking each deed as if in a
furnace. Bread is baked so that people may be
nourished by it and be able to live. So, too, the will is
the strength of the whole work, for it starts by
kneading it and when it is firm adds the yeast and
pounds it severely; and thus, preparing the work in
contemplation as if it were bread, it bakes it in
perfection by the full action of its ardor, and so
makes a greater food for humans in the work they do
than in the bread they eat. A person stops eating
from time to time, but the work of his will goes on in
him till his soul leaves his body. And in whatever
different circumstances the work is performed . . .
it always progresses in the will and in the will comes
to perfection.

HILDEGARD VON BINGEN,
German (1098-1179),
translated by Mother Columba Hart
and Jane Bishop

Mont Blanc, France

TERCE

Action is for the sake of contemplation, the active for
the sake of the contemplative. To labor is to pray.
Work is the discipline (the yoga) by means of which
"body holds its noise and leaves Soul free a little."
Recreation is for the sake of work. Leisure time is for
the sake of recreation – in order that the laborer may the
better return to work. Games are like sleep – necessary
for the health of body and mind – a means to health, the
health of the workman, the laborer, the man who prays,
the contemplative. Leisure is secular, work is sacred.
Holidays are the active life, the working life is the
contemplative life. The object of leisure is work.
The object of work is holiness.

ERIC GILL,
English (1882-1940)

Old City, Jerusalem, Israel

SEXT

Oh the happy ending, the happy ending
That the fugue promised, that love believed in,
That perfect star, that bright transfiguration,

Where has it vanished, now that the music is over,
The certainty of being, the heart in flower,
Ourselves, perfect at last, affirmed as what we are?

The world, the changing world stands still while lovers
kiss,
And then moves on – what was our fugitive bliss,
The dancer's ecstasy, the vision, and the rose?

There is no ending – steps of a dance, petals of flowers
Phrases of music, rays of the sun, the hours
Succeed each other, and the perfect sphere
Turns in our hearts the past and future, near and far,
Our single soul, atom, and universe.

KATHLEEN RAINE,
Irish

Nagarkot, Nepal

NONE

The soul can go voluntarily into the future through the performance of certain rituals, or the soul can go into the future through the medium of death, the death of the body in this world. It is quite possible for a person to send his or her soul into their future to learn of something that is yet to happen and then to bring back that knowledge to the present and use it as a basis for taking action to avoid that occurrence which has been seen in the future. Because the future can be changed – it is not static any more than the present is. With one action taken today you can initiate a whole series of actions in the future and with one action avoided today, you can stop many actions in the future.

VUSAMAZULU CREDO MUTWA,
Zulu

Jogjakarta, Indonesia

VESPERS

When I see nothing annihilated (in the works of God)
and not a drop of water wasted, I cannot suspect the
annihilation of souls, or believe that He will suffer
the daily waster of millions of minds ready made that
now exist, and put Himself to the continual trouble
of making new ones. Thus, finding myself to exist in
the world, I believe I shall, in some shape or other,
always exist; and, with all the inconveniences human
life is liable to, I shall not object to a new edition of
mine, hoping, however, that the *errata* of the last
may be corrected.

BENJAMIN FRANKLIN,
American (1706-1790)

Block Island, Rhode Island

COMPLINE

We shall not cease from exploration
And the end of all our exploring
Will be to arrive where we started
And know the place for the first time.
Through the unknown, remembered gate
When the last of earth left to discover
Is that which was the beginning;
At the source of the longest river
The voice of the hidden waterfall
And the children in the apple-tree
Not known, because not looked for
But heard, half-heard, in the stillness
Between two waves of the sea.
Quick now, here, now, always –
A condition of complete simplicity
(Costing not less than everything)
And all shall be well and
All manner of things shall be well
When the tongues of flames are in-folded
Into the crowned knot of fire
And the fire and rose are one.

> T. S. ELIOT,
> *American (1888-1965)*

South Seas

BECOMING THE CIRCLE

When I was a boy, my Father told me stories. His eyes lit up with an unmistakable passion for history, for other ways of seeing the world. His words conveyed an excitement that transported me from now into then, bringing it to life. Above all, he invoked the experience of human beings who had once lived. He cared deeply for these people from a distant time, wondered what they felt, what they suffered and feared, who they loved, what they dreamed. He gave me a vivid, immediate sense of what their day-to-day lives must have been like. In my mind's eye, my life's time converged with theirs, within the story's altered time, becoming something else.

Among my Father's gifts to me was that of a burning curiosity to experience firsthand what life was like in other worlds, in this and other times. The beckoning distance set me off on years of travels when other paths might have seemed far more prudent. My young man's yearning to experience a sense of the world, and, in the words of Herman Hesse, "to merge my own insignificant life into the infinite and the eternal," had the effect of opening a door which can never be closed.

In my journeys, even in the most remote areas, in virtually every culture of the world, I found a consistent kindness and hospitality toward the wanderer who came with open hands and open mind, a common set of patterns of human engagement. As I spent more time in the world's many traditions, their elements began to merge into one another. Within the many unique ways of coping with life on this Earth, fundamental patterns clearly shone through. There emerged the underlying rhythms of the land, of human interaction, of the cycles of nature, of life and death. The joy of a newborn child; the labor of subsistence; the basic need for food, warmth and shelter, for protection of family. The tenderness of love; the laughter and comfort of friendship; the satisfaction of achieve-ment; the outrage of injustice; the pain of loss; the consolation of belief and the wisdom of acceptance. The incredible power inherent in the will to live, despite heavy odds. At times it seemed that I was traveling in a capsule, insulated from what was around me by a cultural and economic shell that seemed impenetrable. At other times, I experienced such a keen compassion and synchronicity with these people, some of whom were struggling to survive, that I saw myself in them. It seemed as if humanity was drawn together by a magnetic force, at once extraordinary and familiar.

I see the world in still images: frozen moments of suspended time. In a photograph one can seek out an expression that can stand for all expressions, a moment that can signify all time. The photographs in this book bear witness that these people have lived upon this Earth, if only for a brief moment in this passing show.

What meaning can this momentary life have, when time is measured geologically? By definition, it is a heartbeat: a look, a fleeting state of grace. These fragments, these shards of existence can only have significance if they are meant to represent something else: tears for all tears, an experience for all experience. The cry that says we lived once, that we were here. That our lives will not be a story untold. That we touched others who lived on after us. That we added some small thread to the texture of this world.

What is a life? What do we leave behind, that can't be worn down by wind, or time, or fire? It is the trace we leave on memory.

ERIC LAWTON
Pacific Palisades, California

NOTES ON THE PHOTOGRAPHS

MATINS: Young Girl in Boat Window, Mandalay, Burma (now Myanmar), 1976

Rudyard Kipling's "Road to Mandalay" is actually a river, the Irriwaddy of Myanmar. I rose before dawn from a fitful, humid sleep to board a local boat for a long day's journey down the river from Mandalay to Pagan. As first light warmed the damp, wood-framed windows, I looked out and saw, next to me, this Burmese girl, lost in the endless stream of ancient temples that lined the passing shore.

LAUDS: Mother & Child, Imperial Palace, Beijing, China, 1988

I had come to China to find my mother's childhood home. The first day I was in Beijing, I went to meet with her friend who would give me a map with the old street names. I found my way to the Forbidden City, and on to the grounds of the Imperial Palace. I was struck by the elemental presence of thousands of years of history, interwoven into this place. I watched the changing shadows reflected in the water of the pond, cast by the sun's march across the sky, selecting the recipients of its light, as it had countless times in this place.
I turned away, turned back, and saw this.

PRIME: Fisherman at Red Dawn, Santa Monica, California, 1993

Time can seem to move at different rates in different places. At this site one hundred years ago was "The Long Wharf," a mile-long pier which at that time was the major unloading point for what was then the port of Los Angeles. All that remains is a stump of track and a small stone monument.

TERCE: Living Goddess of Kathmandu, Kathmandu, Nepal, 1976

The Palace of the Living Goddess overlooks Durbar Square in the heart of Kathmandu. This young girl was selected from many others because it was found by ancient means that the Goddess of Young Girls resided within her. She lived inside the palace walls and could only go out in public while carried on the shoulders of her "protectors." Tradition held that when this girl reached puberty the Goddess left her body for that of another child, and she was returned to the population as a normal person.

SEXT: Funeral Pyre, Bhaktapur (near Kathmandu), Nepal, 1976

I sat for an afternoon on the bank of the river, watching the gentle way in which these people dealt with that inevitable human experience which all cultures have in common. There was a different tone to their manner from that of the Western world. There was a sadness, but also an inherent sensibility to this process, a palpable feeling that something had been lost, and something had not.

NONE: Gabe, at Watch on the "Seaview," at sea in the Bahamas, 1988

We were at sea on an underwater archeological expedition, searching for a 17th century Spanish galleon that had been wrecked on the shallow Bahamian shoals while returning to Spain, laden with a portion of the spoils of the Incan Empire. Over the ship's radio we had just learned of an approaching Hurricane, which made for a memorable night.

VESPERS: Tibetan Monk, Tibetan refugee camp, near Pokhara, Nepal, 1985

In the foothills of the Annapurna Trail, this Tibetan monastery is the present dwelling place of a wise and gentle people who have learned, all too well, the meaning of impermanence and transition.

COMPLINE: Turkana Mother and Boys, near Loeyangalani, Lake Turkana, Kenya, 1977

In Kenya's Northern Frontier District, near the desert borders of Somalia and Ethiopia, Lake Turkana stretches for 180 miles of green waters known as the Jade Sea, surrounded by a volcanic moonscape. Its inhabitants include the El Molo tribe, which lives on a tiny, rock-strewn island, without a blade of grass or a trace of shade, and raked by a relentless wind. The lake contains Nile perch which reach 300 pounds, and innumerable massive crocodiles. Near to this area, paleontologists found "Lucy," one of mankind's most remote forbears.

MONDAY

MATINS: Mother & Children on Winding Road, near Yangshuo, China, 1988

Just north of Vietnam, this area of southern China is filled with classic karst mountainscapes. A tapestry of ethnic tribespeople have lived from this land for centuries.

LAUDS: Boys by Sea, Huahine, Tahiti 1976

I had arrived in Tahiti, a refugee from a high-rise life in Los Angeles, to commence what turned out to be a three-year journey around the world. Tahiti's tranquil lifestyle, governed by the natural cycles of the day, was a perfect tonic

PRIME: Fisherman, outside Elsinore Castle, Elsinore, Denmark, 1986

Just outside Hamlet's castle, the focal point of Denmark for over a thousand years. The forbidding March wind swept across the frozen North Sea, cutting easily through any attempt at warmth. This man was very committed to the need to fish that day.

TERCE: Young Woman in Doorway, Oaxaca, Mexico, 1981

Among Oaxaca's treasures is Monte Alban, one of the world's great pyramid complexes, which sits atop a plateau overlooking Oaxaca's Spanish Colonial plaza. Indian villages in the surrounding areas are known for the beauty of their ceramic art.

SEXT: Two Survivors, Old City, Jerusalem, Israel, 1977

The Old City of Jerusalem has been dream, sanctuary, inspiration and grave to countless passing souls. Some have sacrificed immensely in order to get here, and to stay here.

NONE: Young Boy in My Mother's Childhood
Home, Tienjin, China, 1988

*In 1988 I realized my lifelong dream of journeying to
China in search of my Mother's childhood home. In the
early part of the 20th century, she had lived with her
family in Tienjin (then called Tientsin), where my
grandfather was with the English-language North China
Star. After a series of adventures and disappointments, I
managed to find the home, much changed by the
ravages of 70 years of turbulent history. This young
boy – the same age as my mother when she lived
there – lived in the house now, and his family
welcomed me inside.*

VESPERS: Young Woman Hiding Face, Tokyo,
Japan, 1976

*This young woman was part of the postwar generation
in Japan that was struggling to find its identity in the
transition from traditional practices to contemporary
life.*

COMPLINE: Young Monk with Mandala,
Thimpu, Bhutan, 1985

*In an extended journey in 1985 to the Himalayan
territories of Darjeeling, Sikkim, Nepal and Bhutan,
I sought out Tibetan monasteries in order to experience
their concentrated presence. This young monk, who
befriended me, helped me to gain insight into a small
part of their tradition and accumulated wisdom.*

..

TUESDAY

MATINS: Man Walking in Forest,
Big Bear, California, 1990

*It is said that the forest will speak forever to those who
will look at it with inner eyes.*

LAUDS: Fishermen at Pont Neuf,
Paris, France, 1972

*My first journey to Europe as a young man was a
revelation. I wandered for hours at a time, fascinated by
the monuments, but even more so by the small, familiar
tokens of a coexistence over time. Pieces of straw
embedded in the mortar between the stones of a Roman
wall, placed there by someone just like me, but two
thousand years ago. The shapes and shadows of the
landscape; the quality of light; the temperature and
taste of the air. I was walking slowly in a timeless dawn
along the Seine when I saw these men, doing what had
always been done at this place.*

PRIME: Young Bhutanese Girl,
Enchey Monastery, Gangtok, Sikkim, 1985

*This girl had come to Enchey Monastery to study and to
train. It was abundantly clear that she was an
extraordinary person.*

TERCE: Three People Moving,
Temple of Heaven, Forbidden City,
Beijing, China, 1988

*Within the area of the Temple of Heaven, for centuries
the Emperors had walked these pathways, away from
the outside world.*

SEXT: Momentary Prince & Princess, Guanajuato, Mexico, 1981

The narrow canyon town of Guanajuato is reached from an underground road, carved from the living stone by an extinct subterranean river. I arrived to find a surreal festival in which all the children of the town were in costume and in character. These two children were the center of it all.

NONE: Young Girl, Thimpu, Bhutan, 1985

One of the glories of travel is that it enables us to encounter, often in the most unlikely places, remark- able beings.

VESPERS: Monk Contemplating Waterfall (Taki), Kinkakuji Temple, Kyoto, Japan, 1976

Kyoto inspires dreams: it is one of those eternal places that has an effect on one's life. Its essential grace is the manifestation of the purity of beauty. In Zen, everything, even a leaf of grass, expresses ultimate reality. In this temple, there is a Zen poem on the quietness of nature entitled: "Scripture Without Words."

COMPLINE: Rickshaw Driver, Deep Night in Kathmandu, Nepal, 1985

The rickshaw driver deftly negotiated the narrow lanes of Kathmandu at 3 a.m., peddling through lights and shadows, the streets and squares alive even at that hour with the rhythmic song of the harmonium and the obscure chant of an ancient storyteller, casting his spell over a transfixed crowd.

WEDNESDAY

MATINS: Kalu Rinpoche, Sonada Monastery, Darjeeling, 1985

The senior Meditation Master of the Kagyu sect of Tibetan Buddhism, Kalu Rinpoche was (and, some say, still is) a kind and patient teacher, a gifted writer and a profound communicator of the ancient traditions and wisdom.

LAUDS: Boatman, Li River, near Yangshuo, China, 1988

Down the Li River from Guilin to Yangshuo, the cormorant fisherman moved along the river in timeless cycles.

PRIME: Men Facing Sea, Asilomar, California, 1982

Asilomar's pines and wind-swept cypresses cast a stark form along the sea, near to Steinbeck's Monterey, California.

TERCE: Woman in Prayer, Mandalay Hill, Mandalay, Burma, 1976

Mandalay Hill is reached after a lengthy climb. This woman was kneeling before a large standing Buddha, its right arm outstretched and pointing, its ceramic ivory surface reflecting the morning light.

SEXT: Dancer 1, Los Angeles, California, 1981

The Art of Dance is to express, through a gesture, the joy and sorrow of existence.

NONE: Woman in Fog Cave,
Huangshan, China, 1988

For thousands of years, Huangshan has been a source of inspiration for artists, writers and pilgrims drawn to its craggy cliffs and fog-shrouded trees. The ascent is made by climbing over 10,000 stone steps carved from the mountainside.

VESPERS: Hands, Santa Monica, California, 1982

A hand can be a thousand things:
The dancer's paintbrush;
The writer's vehicle;
The warrior's weapon;
The lover's touch;
The worker's tool;
The mute's voice;
The aged person's last connection,
and the child's first encounter with the world.

COMPLINE: Mayan Woman with Infant and
Young Girl, Yucatan
(near Chichen Itza), Mexico, 1982

In the jungle of the Yucatan Peninsula, this family lived in a tiny village near the ancient Mayan pyramid of Chichen Itza.

THURSDAY

MATINS: Man in Canoe, Baidam Lake,
Pokhara, Nepal, 1985

In the early mornings I would swim across this lake with an Australian friend. As we would return to this shore, the clouds would part and the great peaks of the Himalayas would be reflected in the glassy waters which surrounded us.

LAUDS: Farmer, near Yangshuo,
China, 1988

Near the karst rock formations unique to this area of southern China, an immense boulder stood at the head of a canyon. In the middle of this rock was a giant hole, over 50 feet wide, that had been carved clear through the solid stone by countless centuries of winds. This man worked the terraced hillsides to feed his family, as his ancestors before him had done, for as long as those winds had blown.

PRIME: Light Through Trees, Huangshan, China, 1988

In the 1920s, my grandfather would seek refuge from the pressures of the newspaper business by coming to Huangshan Mountain to ascend the ancient path to Yu Ping Lu. In early times, this site had been The Temple of the Boddhisattva of Wisdom. When I went there, 68 years later, I set out to trace his footsteps, to seek the things he sought.

TERCE: El Molo Boy, El Molo Island,
Lake Turkana, Kenya, 1977

My three friends and I reached El Molo Island by wading across a waist-deep strait in Lake Turkana, which — we were told — was infested with crocodiles. I thought I would be safest by taking the last spot in the single file line, thinking that if anyone in the front was hit by a crocodile, I could sprint back to shore. I later found out that when the local people crossed the strait, they put their oldest and most infirm at the end of the line, because the crocodiles always hit the end first. This boy is outside one of the only "structures" on the tiny island, a thatched hut made from the straw and dried weeds of the lake. Standing next to him, another El Molo man was painted all over his body in bright white dots. It was his time to perform a rite of passage: to hunt and slay a hippo with a spear, while standing on a thatched raft.

SEXT: My Wife, My Child,
Los Angeles, California, 1992

Gail and Rebecca, just after they made me a father, as we entered our greatest adventure.

NONE: Two Men Playing French Horn Duet under
Pont Neuf, Paris, France, 1983

One of the world's greatest acoustic halls, the underside of this famous stone bridge echoed the music and wit of Paris, and scattered it over the passing waters of the Seine.

VESPERS: Sadhu (Holy Man),
Bhaktapur, Nepal, 1976

This man had walked for thousands of miles on pilgrimage from India to Nepal, with only the clothes on his back. According to custom, people along the way gave him water, food and shelter, out of respect for his holiness and devotion.

COMPLINE: Old Woman with Blue Wall,
Peru, 1987

The Indian villages of central Peru predate the Incas. Spanish conquistadores laid waste to this magnificent empire, but the spirit and resilience of these people enabled them to survive.

FRIDAY

MATINS: Dancer 2, Los Angeles, California, 1981

Just as the wind cannot be seen unless it employs some form to manifest it, a great dancer can disappear within the current of inspired movement.

LAUDS: Old Woman Reading Book,
Taxco, Mexico, 1980

The silver cities of Taxco, Cuernavaca and San Miguel de Allende evoke the flavor of old Mexico. In the steep hillside village of Taxco, every walkway is almost vertical.

PRIME: Man with Prayer Shawl,
Judean Desert, Israel, 1998

We had climbed for hours from En Gedi at the Dead Sea, along a narrow, precipitous path called "The Ascent of the Essenes" (the creators of the Dead Sea Scrolls). We slept under a night sky overflowing with stars, on a plateau known as Chever. As dawn broke, revealing one of the most amazing skies I have ever seen, one of my companions drew a prayer shawl and a bible from his backpack, and stood to give appropriate respect to the power that infuses this ancient land.

TERCE: Pond, Palace of Fine Arts,
San Francisco, California, 1997

Built for the World's Fair at the turn of the 19th Century, San Francisco's Palace of Fine Arts is the last vestige of an age of grace and wonder.

SEXT: Old Woman with Face Tattoos,
Central Taiwan, 1976

In central Taiwan, this woman is from an aboriginal caucasian tribe.

NONE: Bedouin on Camel,
near Jebel Musa, Sinai Desert, 1977

The winding labyrinths of the Sinai make it understandable how the Israelites could have been lost for 40 years. Near to this site is the mountain called Jebel Musa, thought to be Mount Sinai.

VESPERS: Man in Canoe in Jungle River,
Taman Negara Jungle, Malaysia, 1976

The jungle of Taman Negara in Eastern Malaysia provides no lack of adventure. Any number of animals (and the most remarkable insects) inhabit these waters and this dense jungle.

COMPLINE: Night Festival in Siliguri,
Siliguri, India, 1985

Near the border of India and Bhutan, this night festival was filled with the sounds of animated voices and music blended with the smell of incense and perfumes. The myriad colors of the bangles reflected in the candlelight.

SATURDAY

MATINS: Jallikatu (Bull Catching Festival),
near Madurai, Southern India, 1977

The Jallikatu is a centuries-old festival in which the object is to catch a brahma bull by its shoulder hump while it is running at full speed, then ride it for as far as possible on its terrified dash through the screaming crowd. This older, white-haired man was, far and away, the bravest of all assembled, as he rode virtually every bull released down the pathway. None of the younger men whose arms were outstretched really wanted any part of the bulls. In ancient times, the bravest rider was allowed to marry the local princess.

LAUDS: Three Men at Sunrise,
India, 1977

On a dusty train journey, third class, across the width of India from Madras to Bombay. Thirty hours on a wooden seat. Just before dawn, we stopped briefly at a small station somewhere in the middle of India. I gazed wearily into the darkness and was perplexed to see three sets of small, shining lights, swaying below me. As the sun broke the horizon, I realized that I was looking into the eyes of these men, who were looking back at me in silence. And then the train pulled out.

PRIME: Man with Scythe,
Mont Blanc, France, 1978

Just outside the Mont Blanc tunnel linking Italy and France, these mountains and fields have fed people for generations.

TERCE: Woman on Steps, Old City,
Jerusalem, Israel, 1978

In the narrow passageways of the Old City of Jerusalem. I was working on an archeological dig at the southern wall of the Temple Mount. At dawn, I would jog through the vacant passageways of the Old City, on my way to the site where I would begin my work. As the day began, the call to prayers of the muezzin would echo over the "city of stones and bones," and the ancient walkways would come to life.

SEXT: Boy at Sunrise over Mount Everest,
Nagarkot, Nepal, 1976

I walked from Kathmandu before dawn to the top of a hill in Nagarkot, to watch the sunrise over Mount Everest. As I waited, huddling in the cold, I was surprised to see a bright spot of light, exactly opposite from the direction of the rising sun. As the sky lightened, I realized that I was seeing the snowy peak of Everest, the top of the world, catching the first rays of the morning sun. I then looked down and saw this young boy, who had been standing in the darkness, watching me the entire time.

NONE: Boy on Bicycle, Jogjakarta, Indonesia, 1976

I had come to the bustling town of Jogjakarta on the island of Java to see the ancient temple complexes of Prambanan and Borubudur. The look in this boy's eyes has stayed with me for the last twenty-three years.

VESPERS: North Light, Block Island,
Rhode Island, USA, 1995

For over one hundred years the North Lighthouse of Block Island has stood sentinel over the blue waters along Rhode Island's coast. Graceful hotels built of wood have survived to carry on the elegant traditions of the 19th Century.

COMPLINE: Old Man on Boat with Rainbow,
South Seas, 1981

It is believed that the early Polynesians arrived by sea, in ocean-going canoes, navigating by only two stars. It is fascinating to speculate about what must have gone through their minds as they journeyed into the unknown.

CREDITS

Grateful acknowledgement is made to the following publishers and individuals for material reprinted in *The Soul Aflame* :

JAMES AGEE, "Knoxville: Summer 1915," from *A Death in the Family* by James Agee. Copyright © 1957 by The James Agee Trust, renewed 1985 by Mia Agee. Used by permission of Grosset & Dunlap, Inc., a division of Penguin Putnam Inc.

DELMIRA AGUSTINI, "Another Lineage," from *Love Poems from Spain & Spanish America*. Selected and translated by Perry Higman. Copyright © by Perry Higman. Published by City Lights. Reprinted by permission of City Lights.

NADIA BOULANGER, from *Mademoiselle: Conversations with Nadia Boulanger* (with Bruno Monsaingeon), translated by Robyn Marsack. Manchester, England: Carcanet Press, 1985.

AL-GHAZZALI, *Confessions*. Translated by Claud Field. London, 1909.

AMERGIN (attributed), "I am the wind," translated by Douglas Hyde, cited by Kathleen Hoagland, editor. *1000 Years of Irish Poetry*. Old Greenwich, CT: The Devin-Adair Company, 1968.

Quote by HELEN MAYBELL ANGLIN, owner of the Soul Queen restaurant, from the *Chicago Sun–Times, December, 1994*.

ANONYMOUS, "I think over again my small adventures," cited in *World Poetry: An Anthology of Verse from Antiquity to our Time*. Katharine Washburn and John S. Major, editors. Clifton Fadiman, General editor. New York; W. W. Norton & Company, 1998.

MARCUS AURELIUS, "Honor," from *Meditations*. Translated and with an introduction by Maxwell Staniforth. Penguin Books, 1964. Copyright © 1964 by Maxwell Staniforth.

BLACK ELK, excerpt from *The Sacred Pipe: Black Elk's Account of the Seven Rites of the Oglala Sioux*. Recorded and edited by Joseph Epes Brown, Norman, OK: University of Oklahoma Press, 1953.

JAMES BROUGHTON, excerpt from *Gay Soul*, edited by Mark Thompson. HarperSanFrancisco, 1994.

GAUTAMA SIDDHARTHA BUDDHA, excerpts from *Buddha's Teachings*. Juan Mascaro, editor and translator from the Pali. New York: Penguin Books, 1973.

PO CHU-I, "At night," translated by Arthur Waley, from *Translations from the Chinese*. New York: Alfred A. Knopf, Inc. "A Dream of Mountaineering," translated by Arthur Waley, from *One Hundred Seventy Chinese Poems*. Copyright © 1919 and renewed 1947 by Arthur Waley. Reprinted by permission of Alfred A. Knopf, Inc.

EMILY DICKINSON, "Exultation is the going." Reprinted by permission of the publishers and the Trustees of Amherst College from *The Poems of Emily Dickinson*, Thomas H. Johnson, ed. Cambridge, MA: The Belknap Press of Harvard University Press. Copyright © 1951, 1955, 1979, 1983 by the President and Fellows of Harvard College.

ANNIE DILLARD, excerpt from *Pilgrim at Tinker Creek*. New York: Bantam Books, Inc., 1974. Used with permission of the author.

LALLA, "The soul, like the moon," translated by Coleman Barks. Copyright © 1992 by Coleman Barks. Published by Maypop Books, 196 Westview Dr. Athens, GA. 30606. Reprinted with permission of Coleman Barks.

PAUL LAURENCE DUNBAR, "Passion and Love," cited in *The Erotic Spirit: An Anthology of Poems of Sensuality, Love, and Longing*, edited by Sam Hamill. Boston & London: Shambhala Publications, 1996.

ALBERT EINSTEIN, excerpt from *The World as I See It*. Translated by Alan Harris. New York: The Wisdom Library, 1949.

T. S. ELIOT, excerpt from "Little Gidding" in *Four Quartets*, copyright 1942 by T. S. Eliot and renewed

1970 by Esme Valerie Eliot, reprinted by permission of Harcourt, Inc.

ARETHA FRANKLIN, from VH1, June 1991.

BENJAMIN FRANKLIN, excerpt from *The Papers of Benjamin Franklin,* edited by Leonard W. Labaree. New Haven, CT: Yale University Press, 1950.

JACK GILBERT, "The Great Fires." From *The Great Fires: Poems 1982 - 1992* by Jack Gilbert. Copyright © 1992 by Jack Gilbert. Reprinted by permission of Alfred A. Knopf, Inc.

ERIC GILL, excerpt from *A Holy Tradition of Working.* Stockbridge, MA: The Lindisfarne Press, 1983.

MARTHA GRAHAM, "There is a vitality," excerpt from a letter to Agnes De Mille. Cited in *Martha Graham — An Autobiography: Blood Memory.* New York: Washington Square Press, 1991.

SHAMS-UD-DIN MUHAMMAD HAFIZ, "I don't want to be the only one here," in *The Subject Tonight is Love.* Versions by Daniel Ladinsky. North Myrtle Beach, SC: Pumpkin House Press, 1996. Reprinted with permission by Pumpkin House Press.

ROBERT HENRI, excerpt from *The Art Spirit.* Philadelphia and New York: J. B. Lippincott Company, 1960.

HILDEGARD OF BINGEN, "For the will is like a fire. . ." (Part I, Vision 4, Number 21; Scivias 121-122). Reprinted from *Hildegard of Bingen: Scivias,* translated by Mother Columba Hart and Jane Bishop. Copyright © 1990 by the Abbey of Regina Laudis: Benedictine Congregation Regina Laudis of the Strict Observance, Inc. Used by permission of Paulist Press.

JAMES HILLMAN, excerpt from *Insearch: Psychology and Religion.* Dallas: Spring Publications, 1967. Copyright © 1967 by James Hillman. First printing of revised edition 1994 by Spring Publications, Inc. Used by permission of the publisher.

ALICE O. HOWELL, in *The Dove in the Stone: Finding the Sacred in the Commonplace.* Wheaton, IL: Quest Books, 1988.

NIKOS KANZANTZAKIS, excerpt from *Zorba the Greek.* Translated by Carl Wildman. New York: Ballantine Books, 1952.

MARTIN LUTHER KING, JR., excerpt from "I Have A Dream," from *A Testament of Hope: The Essential Writings and Speeches of Martin Luther King, Jr.* Edited by James M. Washington. New York: HarperSanFrancisco, 1991.

GARY KOWALSKI, excerpt from *The Souls of Animals.* Walpole: Stillpoint Press, 1991. Reprinted with permission from Stillpoint Publishing.

MIRABAI, "O friend, understand the body," by Mirabai, translation © Jane Hirshfield, 1994. First appeared in *Women in Praise of the Sacred: 43 Centuries of Spiritual Poetry by Women,* edited by Jane Hirshfield. New York: Harper Collins, 1994. Used by permission of Jane Hirshfield.

WASHINGTON MATHEWS, from *Navojo Legends,* 1897.

SUSAN L. MITCHELL, "Immortality," cited by Kathleen Hoagland, editor. *1000 Years of Irish Poetry.* Old Greenwich, CT: The Devin-Adair Company, 1968.

VUSAMAZULU CREDO MUTWA, edited by Stephen Larsen. *Song of the Stars: The Lore of a Zulu Shaman.* Barrytown: Station Hill Openings, 1996. Reprinted with permission of the editor.

ORPINGALIK, "Songs," from *Translations from the Inuit,* translated by Tom Lowenstein. Reprinted with permission of the translator.

OLD PAPAGO WOMAN, "In the Great Night," translated by Frances Densmore. From Bureau of American Ethnology, Smithsonian Institution, Bulletin 90.

IRENE RICE PEREIRA, "Ignite the Soul," from *The Poetics of the Form of Space, Light and the Infinite.* Copyright © 1969 by I. Rice Pereira. Cited in *An Artist's Book of Inspiration: A Collection of Thoughts on Art, Artists, and Creativity.* Compiled and Edited by Astrid Fitzgerald. Hudson, NY: Lindisfarne Press, 1996.

PSALM 131, from *The Enlightened Heart* by Stephen Mitchell. Copyright © 1989 by Stephen Mitchell. Reprinted by permission of HarperCollins.

KATHLEEN RAINE, "The Sphere," from *Selected Poems*. Hudson, NY: Lindisfarne Press, 1988.

EDWARD ROSTAND, excerpt from *Cyrano de Bergerac*, translated by Louis Untermeyer. Heritage Books, 1960.

CHRISTINA ROSSETTI, "Birthday," from *Selected Poetry*. London: Faber & Faber, Ltd., 1970.

MEVLANA RUMI, "Love is the astrolabe," translated by Yasar Nuri Ozturk and Richard Blakney from *The Eye of the Heart*. Istanbul: The Redhouse Press, 1988.

ALBERT SCHWEITZER, *Reverence for Life: The Words of Albert Schweitzer*. Compiled by Harold E. Robles. HarperSanFrancisco, 1993.

PERCY BYSSHE SHELLEY, "Asia," from *Prometheus Unbound*. The Heritage Press, 1957.

IZUMI SHIKIBU, "When I think of you," translated by Sam Hamill in *The Erotic Spirit: An Anthology of Poems of Sensuality, Love, and Longing*. Boston & London: Shambala Publications, 1996. Reprinted with arrangement with Shambhala Publications, Inc., Boston.

JOHN STEINBECK, excerpt from *The Grapes of Wrath*. New York: Bantam Books, 1939.

ANNA SWIR, "I Talk to my Body," from *Talking to My Body*. © 1996 by Anna Swir. Translated by Czeslaw Milosz and Leonard Nathan. Reprinted by permission of Copper Canyon Press, P.O. Box 271, Port Townsend, WA 98368.

EXCERPT FROM *THE UPANISHADS*, translated by A. B. Keith, from *History of Sanskrit Literature*. Oxford University Press, 1928. Cited by K. M. Pannikkar, preface to *The Kama Sutra*.

VINCENT VAN GOGH, from *Collected Letters, 1873-1890*. Edited by I. Stone, translated by Johanna van Gogh. New York: New American Library, 1960.

WAFU, "White moth," from *Japanese Haiku*. Translated by the editors of The Peter Pauper Press. Mount Vernon, 1955.

WALT WHITMAN, excerpt from *Leaves of Grass*, ed. Emory Holloway, New York: Doubleday, 1926.

ELIE WIESEL, excerpt from *The Gates of the Forest*. New York: Holt, Rinehart & Winston, 1966. Reprinted by permission of the author.

WILLIAM WORDSWORTH, "Intimations of Immortality from Recollections of Early Childhood," from *Collected Poems*. London: Penguin Books, 1944.

WILLIAM BUTLER YEATS, from "Vacillation." Reprinted with the permission of Simon & Schuster from *The Poems of W. B. Yeats: A New Edition*, edited by Richard J. Finneran. Copyright © 1940 by George Yeats, renewed © 1968 by Bertha Georgie Yeats.

ZE YE (TZU YEH), "All night I could not sleep," translated by Arthur Waley, from *Translations from the Chinese,*. New York: Alfred A. Knopf, Inc. © 1919 and renewed © 1947. Used by permission.Publishers, Inc.

Every effort has been made to obtain permission from the copyright owners of all the works reproduced in this book. This has been a lengthy and complex process. If there have been any omissions of acknowledgements, or any rights overlooked, we will be happy to rectify the errors in future editions.